XB
WAT

D1062039

Emma Watson

BER

1|2018

ST. MARY PARISH LIBRARY
FRANKLIN, LOUISIANA

EMMA WATSON

TALENTED ACTRESS

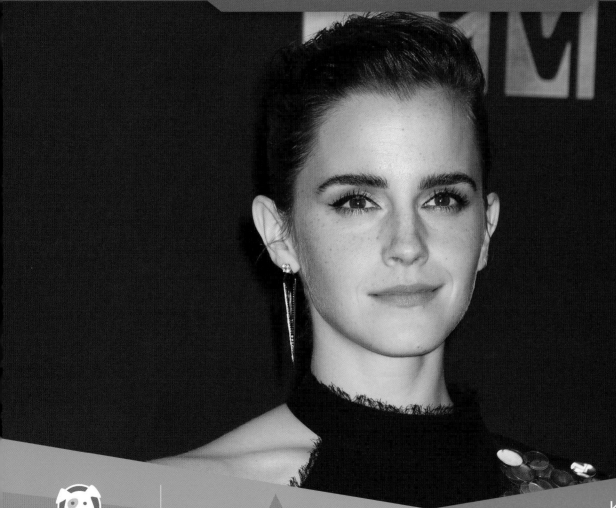

KATIE LAJINESS

Big Buddy Books
An Imprint of Abdo Publishing
abdopublishing.com

BIG BUDDY POP BIOGRAPHIES

abdopublishing.com

Published by Abdo Publishing, a division of ABDO, PO Box 398166, Minneapolis, Minnesota 55439.
Copyright © 2018 by Abdo Consulting Group, Inc. International copyrights reserved in all countries.
No part of this book may be reproduced in any form without written permission from the publisher.
Big Buddy Books™ is a trademark and logo of Abdo Publishing.

Printed in the United States of America, North Mankato, Minnesota.
092017
012018

THIS BOOK CONTAINS
RECYCLED MATERIALS

Cover Photo: PopularImages/DepositPhotos, Inc.
Interior Photos: Alberto Rodriguez/Getty Images (p. 6); ASSOCIATED PRESS (p. 11); Christopher Polk/
    Getty Images (p. 5); Eduardo Munoz Alvarez/Getty Images (p. 25); Frederick M. Brown/Getty
    Images (p. 15); Jason Merritt/Getty Images (p. 21); Jesse Grant/Getty Images (p. 29); Kevin
    Winter/ImageDirect. (p. 13); Kevin Winter/Getty Images (p. 23); Mike Coppola/Getty Images
    (p. 27); Peterspiro/Getty Images (p. 19); Scott Gries/Getty Images (p. 9); Stephen Lovekin/
    Getty Images (p. 17).

Coordinating Series Editor: Tamara L. Britton
Contributing Editor: Jill Roesler
Graphic Design: Jenny Christensen

Publisher's Cataloging-in-Publication Data

Names: Lajiness, Katie, author.
Title: Emma Watson / by Katie Lajiness.
Description: Minneapolis, Minnesota : Abdo Publishing, 2018. | Series: Big buddy pop biographies |
    Includes online resources and index.
Identifiers: LCCN 2017943905 | ISBN 9781532112195 (lib.bdg.) | ISBN 9781614799269 (ebook)
Subjects: LCSH: Watson, Emma, 1990-.--Juvenile literature. | Motion picture actors and actresses--
    Juvenile literature. | Great Britain--Juvenile literature. | United States--Juvenile literature.
Classification: DDC 791.43028092 [B]--dc23
LC record available at https://lccn.loc.gov/2017943905

CONTENTS

RISING STAR

Emma Watson is a famous actress, singer, model, and **activist**. She is best known for her **role** in the Harry Potter movies. Emma is one of today's most popular **entertainers**. She has fans around the world!

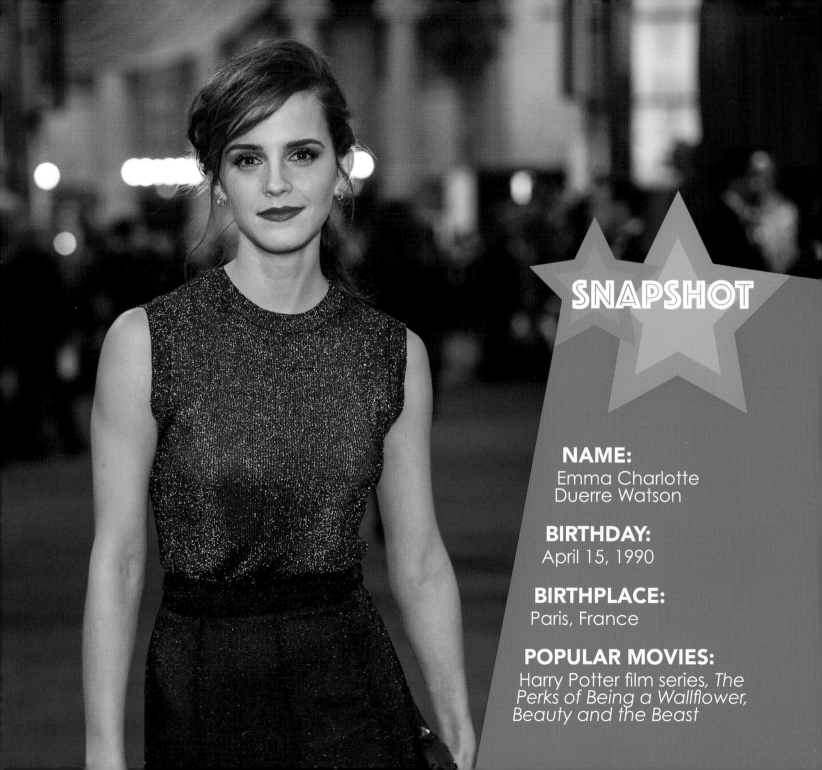

SNAPSHOT

NAME:
Emma Charlotte
Duerre Watson

BIRTHDAY:
April 15, 1990

BIRTHPLACE:
Paris, France

POPULAR MOVIES:
Harry Potter film series, *The Perks of Being a Wallflower*, *Beauty and the Beast*

FAMILY TIES

Emma Charlotte Duerre Watson was born in Paris, France, on April 15, 1990. Her parents are Chris Watson and Jacqueline Luesby. Her younger brother is Alexander. She also has three half **siblings**, Lucy, Nina, and Toby.

Emma and her brother Alex.

WHERE IN THE WORLD?

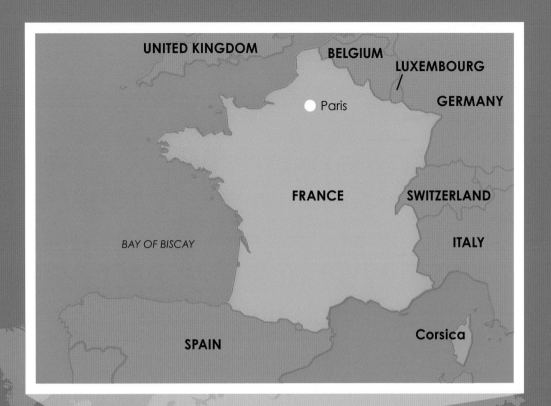

UNITED KINGDOM

BELGIUM

LUXEMBOURG

GERMANY

● Paris

FRANCE

SWITZERLAND

ITALY

BAY OF BISCAY

SPAIN

Corsica

EARLY YEARS

Emma lived in Paris until she was five. Sadly, her parents **divorced**. Emma moved to Oxfordshire, England, with her mother and brother.

At age eight, Emma attended the Dragon School in Oxford, England. She went to the Stagecoach Theater Arts School on Fridays. There, Emma studied the arts.

Growing up, Emma took on small roles in school plays.

HARRY POTTER FAME

DID YOU KNOW ?

The first Harry Potter movie earned more than $974 million in theaters!

In 1999, Emma **auditioned** for a **role** in *Harry Potter and the Sorcerer's Stone*. She got the part of Hermione Granger.

Emma was 11 when the first film came out. Soon, fans began to notice her. She had to get used to her new fame.

Harry Potter author J. K. Rowling wanted Emma for the role of Hermione after her first audition.

Beginning in 2001, a Harry Potter film was **released** about once each year. Much of Emma's life was spent on set. She also traveled the world for **interviews** and film **premieres**. In 2011, the final movie hit theaters.

DID YOU KNOW?

Together, all eight Harry Potter movies have earned more than $6.5 billion!

Actor Rupert Grint *(left)* and producer David Heyman *(center)* worked with Emma on all eight Harry Potter films.

BUILDING A CAREER

Emma worked on other films between the Harry Potter movies. In 2007, she starred in the TV movie *Ballet Shoes*. The next year, Emma was the voice of Princess Pea in *The Tale of Despereaux*.

DID YOU KNOW
The Tale of Despereaux is based on a children's book.

In *The Tale of Despereaux*, Emma plays a lonely princess who befriends Despereaux, a mouse.

TALENTED ACTRESS

In 2011, the Harry Potter series ended. Then, Emma took on new **roles**. In *The Perks of Being a Wallflower*, her character Sam is a spirited teenager.

In *The Perks of Being a Wallflower*, Emma spoke with an American accent.

TOP STUDENT

Just like her character Hermione, Emma earned top grades in school. She began attending the all-girls Headington School in 2003.

While on the Harry Potter set, Emma often studied between scenes. She earned all A's on her final exams.

In 2009, Emma traveled to Providence, Rhode Island. She attended Brown University. There, she got a **degree** in English literature.

Emma graduated from Brown University in 2014.

AWARDS

As a talented actress, Emma has received many **awards**. In 2002, she won a Young Artist Award for her **performance** in *Harry Potter and the Sorcerer's Stone*.

Emma won awards for her other **roles** too. At the 2012 San Diego Film Critics Society Awards, she won Best Supporting Actress for *The Perks of Being a Wallflower*.

Emma won the 2013 People's Choice Award for Favorite Dramatic Actress for her role in *The Perks of Being a Wallflower*.

Emma continued to be a leader. In 2013, she won the Trailblazer **Award** at the MTV Movie Awards. This is given to a leading actor who **inspires** others.

DID YOU KNOW?
The *British GQ* magazine named Emma the 2013 Woman of the Year.

Emma won the 2014 British Artist of the Year award at the BAFTA Los Angeles Britannia Awards. She dedicated her award to her childhood hamster, Millie.

GIVING BACK

Emma enjoyed giving back. She supported equal rights for both men and women. In 2014, she became a Goodwill **Ambassador** for United Nations (UN) Women. Emma has also given speeches for HeForShe, a UN Women's group.

DID YOU KNOW ?

Emma leaves her favorite books in public places for people to discover. She has left them in New York City, New York, and London, England.

In 2016, Emma gave a speech at the UN. She asked everyone to work together for social change.

FASHION ICON

Emma has been known for her style. She also cared about the **environment**. So, Emma often wore clothes that were made without harming the earth.

A natural in front of a camera, Emma has also worked as a model. She has posed for the high-end brands Burberry and Lancôme. From movie **premieres** to magazine covers, Emma has become a fashion icon.

Emma attended the 2016 Metropolitan Museum of Art Costume Institute Benefit Gala in New York City. She wore a dress made from recycled plastic bottles.

BUZZ

DID YOU KNOW ?
In 2017, Emma starred in another movie based on a book, *The Circle*.

In 2017, Emma was very busy. She played Belle in *Beauty and the Beast*. The movie earned $350 million in its first few days!

Emma is successful at everything she tries. Offscreen, her human rights work continues to **inspire** change. Fans are excited to see what Emma does next!

Emma attended the *Beauty and the Beast* premiere in Hollywood, California, with singer Celine Dion *(left)* and actor Dan Stevens *(right)*.

GLOSSARY

activist someone who emphasizes direct action especially in support of or against one side of an issue.

ambassador the job of speaking for, or representing, one country to other countries.

audition (aw-DIH-shuhn) to give a trial performance showcasing personal talent as a musician, a singer, a dancer, or an actor.

award something that is given in recognition of good work or a good act.

degree a title given by a college, university, or trade school to its students for completing their studies.

divorce to legally end a marriage.

entertainer a person who performs for public entertainment.

environment the natural world, including air, water, land, and animals.

inspire to bring about.

interview a meeting in which people talk to each other to ask questions and get information.

performance the act of doing something, such as singing or acting, in front of an audience.

premiere (prih-MIHR) the first time a play, film, or television show is shown.

release to make available to the public.

role a part an actor plays.

sibling a brother or a sister.

ONLINE RESOURCES

Booklinks
NONFICTION NETWORK
FREE! ONLINE NONFICTION RESOURCES

To learn more about Emma Watson, visit **abdobooklinks.com**. These links are routinely monitored and updated to provide the most current information available.

INDEX